LIVES
AND
TIMES

Guy
Fawkes

Rachael Bell

Heinemann
LIBRARY

First published in Great Britain by Heinemann Library
Halley Court, Jordan Hill, Oxford OX2 8EJ,
a division of Reed Educational and Professional Publishing Ltd.
Heinemann is a registered trademark of Reed Educational & Professional Publishing Limited.

OXFORD FLORENCE PRAGUE MADRID ATHENS
MELBOURNE AUCKLAND KUALA LUMPUR SINGAPORE TOKYO
IBADAN NAIROBI KAMPALA JOHANNESBURG GABORONE
PORTSMOUTH NH (USA) CHICAGO MEXICO CITY SAO PAULO

Designed by Ken Vail Graphic Design, Cambridge
Illustrations by Tim Bear
Printed in Hong Kong / China

02 01 00 99
10 9 8 7 6 5 4 3 2

ISBN 0 431 02501 0

This title is also available in a hardback library edition (ISBN 0 431 02499 5)

Some words are shown in bold, **like this**. You can find out what they mean by looking in the glossary. The glossary also helps you say difficult words.

British Library Cataloguing in Publication Data

Bell, Rachael
Guy Fawkes. - (Lives & times)
1. Fawkes, Guy, 1570–1606 - Juvenile literature 2. Revolutionaries - Great Britain - Biography - Juvenile literature 3. Gunpowder Plot, 1605 - Juvenile literature
4. Great Britain - History - James I, - 1603–1625 Juvenile literature
I. Title
941'.061'092

Acknowledgements

The Publishers would like to thank the following for permission to reproduce photographs:

Ashmolean Museum p17; Collections: B Shuel pp20, 21; Crown Copyright: Historic Royal Palaces p23; by kind permission of the Dean and Chapter of York p16; Mary Evans Picture Library pp18, 19; Robert Harding Picture Library: A Woolfit p22

Cover photograph reproduced with permission of e.t. archive.

Our thanks to Betty Root for her comments in the preparation of this book.

Every effort has been made to contact copyright holders of any material reproduced in this book. Any omissions will be rectified in subsequent printings if notice is given to the Publisher.

Contents

The first part of this book tells you the story of
Guy Fawkes.
The second part tells you how you can find out
about his life.

Childhood

Guy Fawkes was **christened** in York. It was April 1570, when Elizabeth I was queen. His parents were Edward and Edith Fawkes.

Guy's father died when he was only nine years old. All that belonged to his father was left to Guy, even though he had a mother and two older sisters.

Growing up

Guy's mother soon married again. The Fawkes family were **Protestants**, but the stepfather was a **Catholic**. Guy soon followed his Catholic beliefs.

It was not easy to become a Catholic in those days. There were laws to try to stop you. Catholic priests were put in prison and people who helped them were punished.

Fighting overseas

When Guy was 21 he received all his father's money. Two years later he left England to join the Spanish army. He wanted to fight for the **Catholic** church.

In 1603, a new king, James I, was crowned. English Catholics were afraid he would be cruel to them. They looked for some Catholic soldiers to help them and found Guy Fawkes.

Fighting at home

They told Guy their **plot**. They wanted to get rid of the king and **parliament** and put **Catholics** in their place. They could blow them all up on November 5th when the king opened parliament.

Guy agreed to help. He knew all about **explosives** so he was perfect for the job. The plotters rented the cellar beneath the parliament building and filled it with barrels of gunpowder.

Caught!

Some plotters sent a letter to their **Catholic** friends in **parliament**. It told them to stay away from the opening on November 5th. But they passed the letter to the king!

James I ordered guards to search the whole parliament building. Guy was caught with **touch paper** in hand, hiding behind the barrels in the cellar!

Hanged

On January 27th, 1606, Guy and 6 others were taken to court. They were found guilty of plotting to kill the king and his **parliament**, and **sentenced** to death.

Four days later, a platform was built opposite the parliament building. There they were all hanged. Guy had to be helped up the ladder because he had been **tortured**.

Clues in writing

How do we know about Guy Fawkes if he lived over 400 years ago? The church kept records of **christenings**. You can still see Guy's record today.

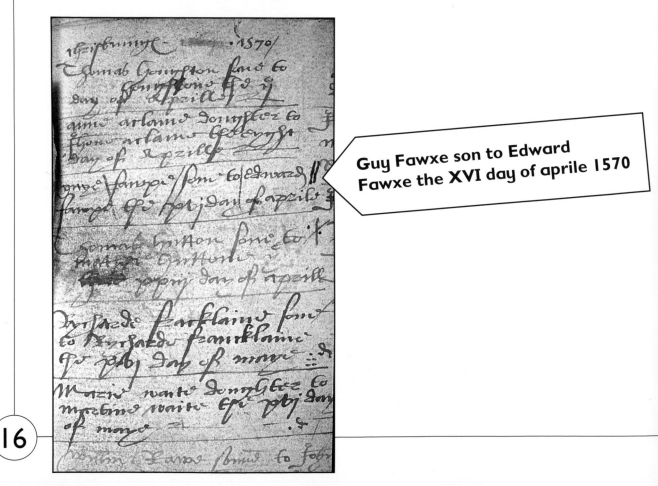

Guy Fawxe son to Edward Fawxe the **XVI** day of aprile 1570

We know how the **plot** went wrong because the warning letter still exists. It was sent to Lord Mounteagle, one of the **Catholics** in parliament.

my lord out of the loue i beare to some of youere freindz i haue a caer of youer preseruacion therfor i would aduyse yowe as yowe tender youer lyf to deuyse some epscuse to shift of youer attendance at this parleament for god and man hathe concurred to punishe the wickednes of this tyme and thinke not slightlye of this aduertisment but retyere youre self into youre contri wheare yowe maye expect the euent in safti for thowghe theare be no apparance of anni stir yet i saye they shall receyue a terrible blowe this parleament and yet they shall not seie who hurts them this councel is not to be contemned becauss it maye do yowe good and can do yowe no harme for the dangere is passed as soonas yowe haue buvnt the letter and i hope god will gine yowe the grace to mak good use of it to whose holy proteccion i comend yowe

To the ryght honorable the Lord Mounteagle

Pictures

We are not sure what Guy looked like. This picture of Guy and the other plotters was drawn in the year he died. We don't know if the artist saw Guy in real life.

Artefacts

Some people believed that
Guy used this lantern in
the dark cellar. It is
now in a museum
in Oxford.

Guy Fawkes' Night

On 5th November 1605, James I ordered special church services to be held, to thank God for his protection. Today, 5th November is still a celebration for many people.

Some people remember Guy Fawkes by asking for 'a penny for the guy'. Most people just get together and enjoy a bonfire and fireworks display.

Buildings

These buildings in York were already old when Guy was a boy. This was a whole street of butchers' shops called The Shambles. What can you buy there now?

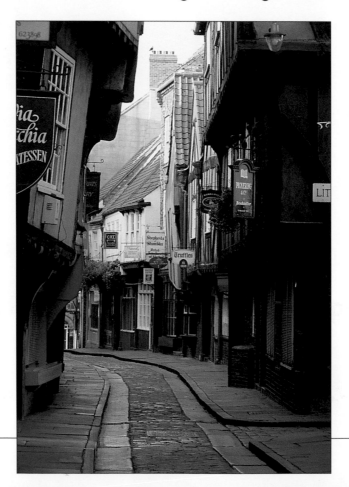

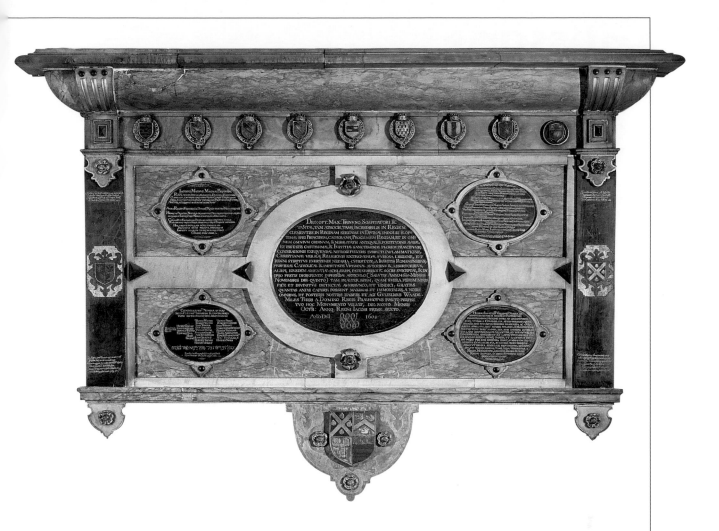

This **plaque** is in the room where Guy was
questioned about the plot after being
tortured. It is in the Tower of London.

Glossary

This glossary explains difficult words, and helps you to say words which are hard to say.

artefacts things which survive from the past that tell us more about it

christened sprinkled with water as a sign of being welcomed into the Christian Church. You say *kris-end*

Catholic Christians who have the Pope in Rome as the head of their church – the Roman Catholic Church

explosives used to blow up buildings or other big things

parliament the group of people chosen to run the country. You say *par-le-ment*

plaque a wall-hanging which tells you about something or someone famous from the past. You say *plark*

plot secret plan

Protestant Christians who do not have the Pope as the head of the church – they broke away from the Roman Catholic Church in the 1500s

sentenced the punishment ordered by the law court

torture putting someone under a lot of cruel pain to make them answer questions – Guy Fawkes was stretched out by his hands and feet on a rack that was pulled tighter and tighter

touch paper special paper used for lighting fires

Index